ON THE JOB

a play by David Fennario

Vancouver, Talonbooks, 1976

copyright © 1976 David Fennario

published with assistance from the Canada Council

Talonbooks
201 1019 East Cordova
Vancouver
British Columbia V6A 1M8
Canada

This book was typeset by Gretchen Amussen of B.C. Monthly Typesetting Service, designed by David Robinson and printed by Hemlock Printers for Talonbooks.

First printing: November 1976

Talonplays are edited by Peter Hay.

Canadian Cataloguing in Publication Data

Fennario, David, 1947-
    On the job

    ISBN 0-88922-102-2 pa.

    I. Title.
PS8561.E5605   C812'.5'4   C76-016036-8
PR9199.3.F

*For Billy Sullivan & Patrick O'Toole,
who were there*

On the Job was first performed at Centaur Theatre in Montréal, Québec, on January 29, 1975, with the following cast:

Billy	Griffith Brewer
Union Boss	Alex Brunhanski
Rene	Edmond Grignon
Jacky	Terry Haig
Gary	Jorma Lindqvist
Jerome	Denis Payne
Shaw	R. D. Reid
Mike	Michael Rudder

Directed by David Calderisi
Designed by Felix Mirbt
Costumes by Diane Johnston
Lighting by Tim Williamson

This same production was taken to the National Arts Centre in Ottawa, Ontario on May 20, 1975 and it was revived at Centaur Theatre in Montréal, Québec on January 29, 1976.

On the Job was also performed at the Arts Club Theatre in Vancouver, British Columbia, on February 25, 1976, with the following cast:

Billy	Jonah Forde
Union Boss	Ron Miller
Rene	Jerry Wasserman
Jacky	Robert Mark Weber
Gary	Bruce Greenwood
Jerome	Sandy Kovack
Shaw	David Berner
Mike	Robert Carey

Directed by Bill Millerd
Designed by Alison Green
Costumes by Linda Morgan
Lighting by Marsha Sibthorpe

*The shipping room of a dress factory in Montreal
on Christmas Eve, 1970.*

*RENE unlocks the shipping room door, puts on
the lights, unlocks the cage door, then settles
down at his desk with his toast and coffee. He
arranges some orders on a rack of dresses, then
JACKY and MIKE enter noisily.*

JACKY:

Yeah, yeah. So Eddy and the guys on the fifth floor
been bitching about this goof for weeks, right?

MIKE:

Ahuh?

JACKY:

Yeah, so I'm checking him out and I'm way ahead of
the goof. I'm wise to his game.

MIKE:

Which goof do ya mean?

They take off their coats and boots.

JACKY:

> Ah, the last of the red hot Pepsi's there. The one in the leather jacket with a million zippers on it.

MIKE:

> Oh yeah, zippers. The one there with the pound of grease.

JACKY:

> Yeah, yeah, greaseball. Struts around like a TV wrestler.

> *BILLY enters.*

> Say, Billy.

BILLY:

> Morning, boys. Morning, Rene.

MIKE:

> Yeah, that guy. Sure. He backed up his truck and knocked Ti-Jean off the dock last week. I was there.

JACKY:

> Yeah, so I'm down on the dock yesterday and greaseball comes up to me waving the invoice. "Sign it," he says. "No fuckin' way," I says. "Hey, hey. Sign it, tabernack" and "No, man," I says, "you bring the stuff upstairs, then I'll sign it."

MIKE:

> Yeah?

JACKY:

> Yeah, so then he makes like he's gonna use some muscle, but he gets nice real quick soon as he sees I'm ready for him. The guy's all mouth.

MIKE:
 So he help ya bring the stuff upstairs, eh?

JACKY:
 Fuckin' right and thanked me when I signed the
 invoice too.

MIKE:
 Too much.

JACKY:
 That's the way to do it, ch, Billy?

BILLY:
 You're sure talking a lot this morning.

JACKY:
 Holiday, Billy. Christmas is coming. Goose is getting
 fat.

> *They relax around the packing table, BILLY*
> *with his coffee thermos and newspaper; JACKY*
> *with coffee and toast; MIKE with Coke, Mae*
> *West cake and comic book.*

 Gimme cigarette, Mike.

> *MIKE passes him one and burps.*

 Aw fuck, Mike. Keep your breakfast to yerself,
 alright? Coke freak.

MIKE:
 Maybe I'll try 7-Up.

JACKY:
 Yeah, do that.

MIKE:
 Hey, so ya backed down greaseball, eh? Did ya do the
 Dead Finger on him?

11

JACKY:
>Naw, I did the Old Toe Jam, then I did the Dead Finger.

>>*JACKY bonks MIKE off the bean with a dead finger.*

MIKE:
>Hey.

>>*JACKY starts fun-hassling MIKE.*

JACKY:
>I did the Toe Jam, then the Dead Finger.

MIKE: *hitting JACKY with his comic book*
>Hey, Jacky. Touche pas. Hey, man.

>>*A loud buzzer sounds. A sudden hum of machinery is heard and the guys line up in front of the packing table. First MIKE staples the boxes, then he hands them to JACKY who packs them. BILLY sits on a stool making up invoices.*

>>*GARY walks in late with a butterfly roll and a coffee.*

JACKY:
>Say, Gary.

GARY:
>Say, guys. What's happening?

>>*He takes a bite of his roll.*

>Ugh, hard as a rock. Fuckin' Irving. Hey, I asked him downstairs if his butterfly rolls are fresh and shure, he says, shure. I just catch them this morning already.

JACKY:
>Yeah, that's Irving alright. Funny with the jokes.

GARY:
>Hey, so we got the afternoon off, eh?

JACKY:
>Yeah, did ya bring in some booze like I told ya?

GARY:
>Yeah, got a bottle here.

RENE:
>Hey, Gary.

JACKY:
>Gonna have some fun, right Mike?

MIKE:
>Yeah, just like last year when Jacky got so stoned he . . .

RENE:
>Hey, Gary. Hey, Boyce.

GARY: *turning around*
>Yeah?

RENE:
>The ears are bad this morning?

GARY:
>No, the ears are good.

RENE:
>Did you punch the clock?

GARY:
>Yeah.

RENE:
> So get to work.

> *GARY keeps drinking his coffee.*

RENE:
> Hey, Boyce, don't fuck around.

GARY:
> Lemme finish my coffee, for Christ's sake.

RENE:
> You don't get paid to drink coffee. Now move.

GARY:
> Aw, fuck.

RENE:
> Come on, get to work.

> *GARY goes over and tosses his coffee and his roll into the trash can with a bang. RENE turns his attention back to his paper work.*

JACKY:
> What's the matter, Rene? Got no tail last night?

RENE:
> Shut up, stupid.

JACKY:
> Got no tail last night, eh?

RENE:
> Shut up stupid and do your work.

JACKY:
> Alright, alright.

MIKE:
> Guess he didn't get any, eh?

14

JACKY:
>Aw, fuck off.

RENE:
>Hey, you guys. Where's the 1411's?

JACKY:
>The what?

RENE:
>The 1411's. Steiner's gonna be here in an hour.

MIKE:
>On the rack.

RENE:
>Where?

JACKY:
>In the back.

MIKE:
>On the rack.

BILLY:
>They're just around the corner, over there.

MIKE:
>In the back.

JACKY:
>On the rack.

RENE:
>Okay, so go get them. Vite, vite. Wake up, wake up.

JACKY: *exiting down the back with MIKE who is singing*
>In the back, on the rack. In the back, on the rack . . .

RENE: *shaking his head*
>Tabernack.

BILLY:
> Holiday.

RENE:
> Everyday's a holiday for them.

> *He looks at one of the boxes on the cart of finished packages.*

> Hey, Gary. Do you know how to write? I can't read this. Do that address again.

> *To BILLY.*

> Last week I got a box back from London . . . London, England.

> *He goes back and sits down at his desk.*
> *JACKY and MIKE enter with a rack of dresses.*

JACKY:
> The foot, Mike. Watch the foot. Here they are, Rene.

RENE:
> So?

JACKY:
> So?

RENE:
> Pack them, tabernack.

MIKE:
> Back, rack, pack. Tabernack. Hey, pack, rack, back, tabernack.

JACKY:
> Fuck off.

Each man performs his work function until
MIKE's stapler breaks down. GARY is standing
next to BILLY addressing the boxes.

MIKE:

Aw, shit. Hey, Rene. You gonna buy me a new
stapler for Christmas?

RENE:

Sure, I'll buy you a dozen so you can break them all.

JACKY:

Yeah, dummy. Write us a letter when you're ready,
alright?

MIKE:

Ever think of helping me?

JACKY:

Never.

He taps BILLY on the shoulder.

Hey, oldtimer. Hear about the queer truck driver who
blew his own horn? Eh? Slow. You're very slow this
morning, Billy. Hey, Gary. Gotta French joke for ya.

GARY:

Later.

JACKY:

Listen, why does a bloke have to take four aspirins
when he's got a headache, eh? One for every corner
of his head.

GARY:

Hey, not too close.

JACKY:

Eh?

GARY:
>Hey, what's with you? Chew on your socks at night?

JACKY:
>Fun-ny. Yours is coming.

RENE: *snatching the stapler from MIKE*
>Hey, Mike. Wake up. Wake up. Like this. Like this.
>Like this. You watching, eh, Sleeping Beauty? Watch.
>Like this.

JACKY:
>Sleeping Beauty. That's a good one, Rene. That's a
>good one.

RENE:
>Like this. Like this.

JACKY:
>Yeah, put him on a stick and make him jump, Rene.
>Make him jump.

>*The telephone on RENE's desk rings.*

RENE: *tossing the stapler at JACKY*
>Here, Mr. Bullshit. You help him and from now on
>you keep on helping him.

>*RENE goes and answers the telephone.*

MIKE:
>Mr. Bullshit. That's a good one, Rene. That's a good
>one.

JACKY:
>What's with Rene?

BILLY:
>Aw, it's that new manager Shaw giving Rene a hard
>time.

18

JACKY:
> Huh?

BILLY:
> Yeah, so take it easy for awhile, okay?

JACKY:
> Huh?

GARY: *singing softly*
>> When I'm dead, bury me deep
>> Down along Saint Antoine Street.

JACKY:
> Wow! Gary's singing.

GARY:
>> Place a brick upon my head
>> And tell all the pretty girls I'm dead.

JACKY:
> Yeah, Mike. So last week I'm down at Joe Beef's on the waterfront. I'm down there with my brother-in-law.

MIKE:
> Oh yeah. Joe Beef's.

JACKY:
> Yeah, and this drag queen is sitting with a sailor and she's saying, "Hands off, honey. Santa Claus is dead. You don't get nothing for nothing no more." Yeah. In Joe Beef's.

MIKE:
> Oh yeah. Joe Beef's.

JACKY:
> Fuck, you're slow this morning, Mike.

> *To GARY.*

JACKY:
Everything else runs at 45. He runs at 33 1/3.

MIKE:
Oh yeah, Joe Beef's. I was there one time.

JACKY:
Fuck, where's the other stapler, Mike?

MIKE:
Dunno. Think the guy from Premier Shirts borrowed it.

RENE: *on the telephone*
Hey, you guys shut up.

JACKY:
Mange lamarde.

MIKE:
Joe Beef's. I was there one time.

JACKY:
Fuck.

RENE:
Hey, Billy. How many 1050's we got there?

BILLY:
1050's?

He looks through his invoices.

Uh, 84.

RENE:
You sure?

BILLY:
Well, that's what it says.

RENE:
> Moudez, taberwit.

> *He exits down the back.*

JACKY:
> You going over to the stock room?

RENE: *yelling from the back*
> Yeah. Answer the phone, eh?

JACKY:
> Yeah, sure. Take your time.

> *He pulls out a bottle of booze.*

> Come on. Hey, let's spread a little peace on earth around.

BILLY:
> It's kind of early, eh?

JACKY:
> Hey, Billy. It's our booze break.

MIKE: *taking a slug from the bottle*
> WOOO! Superior Dress special.

JACKY:
> Wakes ya up, eh, Sleeping Beauty? Kiss, kiss, kiss.

MIKE:
> Hey, fuck off.

JACKY:
> Hey, come on. Gimme a kiss. I wanna turn into a frog.

MIKE:
> Hey, relax. Hey.

GARY: *taking a slug and passing the bottle to BILLY*
Here ya go, Billy.

BILLY:
No, not right now. Can't hold the stuff like I used to.

JACKY:
So who wants to hold it?

GARY: *pulling a bottle out of his work apron*
And I got a bottle of whiskey.

JACKY:
Hey, yeah. Take a walk with Johnny Walker.

There is a burst of laughter from the office.

Sounds like a real joy mob in there.

MIKE:
Office party's starting real early this year.

JACKY:
The salesmen, the models and the secretaries.

MIKE:
And everybody gets the afternoon off.

GARY:
Rene didn't say nothing about that.

JACKY:
Don't have to. We always get Christmas Eve off.
Hey, Beauty, quit hogging that bottle. Hey, watch.

He takes a slug out of the Coke bottle, then a slug of rum. He swishes them both around in his mouth, then swallows.

Ah, rum and Coke.

MIKE:
Hey, can ya do that with ice cubes?

JACKY:
You wanna taste? Eh?

He shakes a dead finger at him.

MIKE:
Hey, don't touch the merchandise.

BILLY: *looking up from his paper*
Any of you guys heard of a Zeke Boucher?

JACKY:
Who?

BILLY:
Here in the paper, Zeke Boucher from Point Saint Charles going up on manslaughter.

MIKE:
Peanuts?

JACKY:
Yeah, Peanuts Boucher. Lemme see that. Where?

BILLY:
There.

MIKE:
What's it say?

JACKY:
Fuckin' Jesus, he went and did it. Stomp some guy to death in a tavern.

MIKE:
Lemme see it.

JACKY: *handing MIKE the paper*

No surprise to me, man. Peanuts always was bad news. You lived in the Point, Gary. You musta heard of him. The guy's a legend down there.

GARY:

Hold it. I'm trying to remember. Uh, did he hang around the pool hall down on Wellington Street?

JACKY:

Naw, not that goof. Peanuts. The Peanuts. The French lad down there.

GARY:

Co-co Lachance?

JACKY:

Naw, Peanuts.

GARY:

Hold it. I'm trying to remember. Did he hang around the pool hall down on Wellington Street?

JACKY:

Yeah, he'd drop by there sometimes.

GARY:

Little guy about yea high with eyes like a barracuda?

JACKY:

Yeah, that's him and man, was he trouble. Sudden death. A fit taker, ya know. Sick in the head. He'd go right strange sometimes and always walked like this. Yeah, like this. Just like a rooster, man. Skinny little runt about yea high, but, man, he could jump six feet in any direction. Walked and looked just like this. And all the time he'd be bouncing, man. Bouncing and just waiting for the wrong word or look from anybody.

24

GARY:
>Had a complex, eh?

JACKY:
>Well, he had something, that's for sure. And he'd kill ya for calling him Zeke and he'd kill ya for calling him Peanuts and he didn't like guys who were taller than him and everybody was taller than him, so, man, you can imagine the complications.

MIKE:
>Hey, I seen him jump two guys on the boardwalk once. Pow. Game over. Two down and one running.

BILLY:
>You make him sound like a hero or something.

JACKY:
>He was alright.

GARY:
>He lived the way he wanted to anyhow.

BILLY:
>The guy was sick. They shoulda locked him up a long time ago.

GARY:
>Sure, he's sick, so lock him up, eh, Billy? Why don't they just kill them when they're born?

BILLY:
>Didn't mean it that way.

JACKY:
>Yeah, he wasn't a smartass or nothing like that, Billy. He just wouldn't take any shit from anybody.

MIKE:
>Yeah, I remember he stood up for me once. He knocked down this guy who was bugging me and . . .

Well, he knocked me down too, but I think he was
helping me. I jut got in the way. It was sort of dark
and . . .

JACKY:

Take a walk, will ya?

GARY:

I remember seeing him in a bar once, sitting alone by
himself.

JACKY:

Always alone, man.

MIKE:

Says here in the paper it was a waiter he killed.

JACKY:

A waiter, eh? The guy musta asked Peanuts for his
I.D. Zeke Boucher, eh? You don't look eighteen?
Don't call me Zeke, est-ti-what? BOOM! One dead
waiter, man.

> *RENE enters. The guys hide their bottles and*
> *scramble back to work.*

MIKE:

Hey, uh, Rene? We're running outta small boxes.

RENE:

Big deal. You been working hard, eh?

JACKY:

Oh, sweat, sweat, sweat.

RENE:

Okay, funny guy. You and Mike bring that cart down
on the dock.

JACKY:

Right.

26

RENE:
> Now.

JACKY:
> Okay, we got two more orders here then . . .

RENE:
> Right now. Move it.

JACKY:
> Hey, don't get excited.

RENE:
> Move it, stupid.

JACKY:
> Hey, who you talking to, man? I don't take that kind of shit, Rene.

RENE:
> Yeah?

JACKY:
> Yeah, try it on somebody else.

RENE:
> Okay, Mr. Thompson, will you please take the cart?

MIKE:
> Come on, Jacky.

JACKY:
> Fuck.

> *JACKY and MIKE exit with the cart.*

RENE:
> And you, Gary. Help Billy with those invoices.

GARY: *softly*
> Fuck you.

RENE exits down the back.

BILLY:
So, how you doing, Gary?

GARY:
Take a guess?

BILLY:
Lousy.

GARY:
Yeah, lousy.

BILLY:
You look a bit hung over.

GARY:
Yeah, I was up late last night.

BILLY:
Rene getting on your nerves, eh?

GARY:
Yeah.

BILLY:
Well, he's too pushy sometimes, but that's his job.
Can't be a foreman and a nice guy.

GARY:
Yeah.

BILLY:
Ignore him when he gets like that. Like Mike.

GARY:
I'm not Mike.

BILLY:

> Didn't say you were. Pass me that pad over here, will
> ya?

GARY:

> That one?

BILLY:

> Yeah, thanks. My legs are really bothering me this
> morning. Shit.

GARY:

> You been here for years, eh, Billy?

BILLY:

> Yeah, five . . . No, six years.

GARY:

> Fuck, man, I've been here six months and I'm going
> crazy.

BILLY:

> You'll get used to it.

GARY:

> What? Going crazy?

BILLY:

> No, the work.

GARY:

> I don't know if I wanna get used to his. I mean, uh,
> how do ya survive a lifetime of shit like this, man?

BILLY:

> Well, you're young. Maybe you can find a good job.

GARY:

> So what happened to you? You're not working here
> 'cause you like it, are ya?

BILLY:

> Nope . . . Automation.

GARY:

> Automation?

BILLY:

> Yeah, that's what happened to me . . . Used to be a
> draftsman. Yeah, good pay.

GARY:

> Laid you off, eh?

BILLY:

> Yeah, not even a thank you. But my kids are grown
> up, so it coulda been worse.

GARY:

> What makes you think I'm gonna be any luckier?

BILLY:

> Well, you're smart . . . sometimes.

GARY:

> Yeah.

BILLY:

> Maybe ya ought to go back to school or something.

GARY:

> Yeah, sure. Ya know what B.A. stands for? Barely
> Able.

BILLY:

> Well, ya got a point there.

GARY:

> Fuckin' right. Forget about philosophy and literature,
> man, they oughta give courses on how to fill out un-
> employment forms. Ten easy ways to get on welfare.

BILLY:

>Well, glad I'm not young anymore.

GARY: *pulling out his bottle*

>Yeah. Well, I'll drink to that.

BILLY:

>Yeah, me, I've got eight years.

GARY:

>Eight years?

BILLY:

>Yeah, then I can get my pension.

RENE:

>Gary. Hey, Gary?

GARY:

>Quite the life.

BILLY:

>It's a living.

RENE:

>Boyce, quit fucking around. Hey, Boyce!

GARY:

>Yeah, yeah, yeah.

>>*GARY exits down the back. JACKY and MIKE enter. JACKY is standing on top of the car and MIKE is pushing it.*

JACKY:

>Superior Dress Express. Left now. Right now. Back up. Back up a little. Left, that's right. No, not right. Left, ya dummy. Left. Okay, straight ahead. Watch the merchandise.

MIKE:
>Watch the merchandise.

>*They park the cart. JACKY pulls a bottle of booze out of a paper bag.*

JACKY:
>Check it out, Billy.

BILLY:
>Jeez, a forty ouncer.

JACKY:
>Yeah, that driver for Fobelmann came across with a gift again this year.

MIKE:
>Yeah, all those little favours we done for him paid off.

JACKY: *taking a slug and passing the bottle to MIKE*
>Woo, we're gonna have a good time holiday.

MIKE:
>Yeah.

>*He takes a slug.*

>Hey, is that Rene coming?

JACKY: *taking another slug*
>Naw, he's just breathing hard.

>*JACKY just has time to hide the bottle as GARY and RENE enter with a rack of dresses. The work process begins again.*

>*The guys sneak a drink while RENE isn't looking and then MIKE and JACKY start singing.*

MIKE
AND JACKY:
>   Oh, you better not shit,
>   You better not shout,
>   You better not fart 'cause
>   You'll blow your brains out.
>   Diarrhea's coming to town.

RENE:
>   Keep it down, keep it down.

JACKY:
>   Hey, Rene. It's jingle bell time, man.

RENE:
>   Yeah. Well, jingle your bells on your own time.

JACKY:
>   Ho, ho, ho.

>   *He takes a slug from his bottle.*

RENE:
>   What's that smell?

JACKY:
>   Yeah, quit farting, Mike.

RENE:
>   Hey, no drinking, eh? You do that after work, under-
>   stand?

SHAW: *from the office door*
>   Rene.

RENE:
>   Yes, sir.

>   *He exits up the stairs through the office door.*

JACKY: *taking a slug and passing the bottle around*
Ummmm, this stuff is going down g-o-o-d, good.
Any of you guys see Judy in that miniskirt the other
day?

GARY:
Judy, the model?

JACKY:
Yeah, the one there with the lungs. Man, would I
love to ball that upside downside round side, all over,
man. Just gimme the chance.

GARY:
Aw, you wouldn't know what to do with it.

JACKY:
Hey, fuck. She'll think she's died and gone to heaven.

GARY:
Chick like that don't ball nothing making less than
two bills a week, man. Better get a raise, Jacky.

JACKY:
Relax, relax. Here, take a slug, man, and spread a
little j-o-y, joy.

MIKE:
Hey, hey.

He sings.

Moma's on the bottom
Poppa's on the top

JACKY joins in.

Sister's in the kitchen
Yelling sock it to her, Pop.

Granny's in the corner
Barfing in a pail
And brother's on a corner
Yelling tail for sale.

Chorus.

Dirty boogie, bop bop,
Bop bop,
Dirty boogie, bop bop,
Bop bop.

Dirty boogie, dirty boogie,
Dirty boogie, dirty boogie,
Dirty boogie,
Bop, bop, bop.

JACKY does an Elvis imitation.

Went down to the basement to get some cider.
Saw a bed bug nailing a spider.
Turn my head, took a look at my cat.
There's my cat going down on a rat.

Dirty boogie, bop bop, etc.

Saw my Daddy
Laying down on the floor
He made some holes,
Now he's making some more.

Dirty boogie, bop bop, etc.

JACKY: *finishing*
A wop bop, a lop bop, a bop bam boom.

GARY:
Wow, too much! Haven't heard that song since I left
the Point.

JACKY:
Aw fuck, I used ta know a million verses to it. Forgot most of them.

BILLY:
Dirty boogie, bop bop.

JACKY:
Come on, Billy. It's your turn.

BILLY:
Aw, that's kid's stuff.

JACKY:
Do that song you did last year?

BILLY:
What song?

MIKE:
That old song about Montreal.

BILLY:
Jesus, I musta been drunk.

GARY:
Here ya go. Wet your whistle.

BILLY: *taking the bottle*
Oh, alright. Uh, okay. Ready?

They all sing together.

Oh, the English they live on Saint George's Street.
The Welsh live in Saint David's Lane.
The Jews are very fond of Craig Street.
And every nation owns The Main.

The Scotch they live on Argyle Avenue.
The French they live in Côte Saint Paul.
But the Irish you can't beat for they own Saint
    Patrick's Street.
Every nation has a street in Montreal.

JACKY:
    Yeah, throw the rest in the canal.

MIKE:
    Hey, hey. I used ta have this skinny chick jumped like
    a rabbit.

JACKY:
    Had teeth like one too.

MIKE:
    Yeah, and boy did she love. I mean l-o-v-e, love to . . .

    RENE and SHAW enter. The guys scramble.

MIKE:
    Hey, Rene. We're right out of those small boxes.

RENE:
    Yeah, yeah.

MIKE:
    Uh, hi. Uh, Mr. Shaw? You guys got a party going up
    there, eh? Ha, ha. Party going. Party. Par . . .

    He coughs.

SHAW: *freezing MIKE out*
    Well, Rene. How much do we have in the 1411's?

RENE: *checking a stock list on a clip board*
    87.

SHAW.
    And the 1050's?

RENE:
> Two racks full. About a hundred.

SHAW:
> About a hundred. Any 1807's left?

RENE:
> Maybe five or six in the back.

SHAW:
> Maybe five or six in the back? Rene, would you please make it a point to know exactly what we have in stock or is that too much to ask?

RENE: *pauses*
> Uh, do you know what's in stock?

SHAW:
> I don't have to know. I'm not the shipper. That's your job. Now, count out the 1050's and 1807's for me. Please. Thank you.

> *RENE exits down the back. SHAW puts the eagle eye on the guys. MIKE gets flustered and wrecks a couple of boxes.*

MIKE:
> Uh, hey. Uh, the guy from Premier Shirts borrowed the other stapler and uh . . .

> *RENE re-enters.*

SHAW:
> Well?

RENE:
> There's ninety-three 1050's and seven 1807's.

SHAW:
> Rene, where is the rest of them?

RENE:

> Of the what?

SHAW:

> The 1050's and 1807's.

RENE:

> There were orders for them last week so I shipped
> them.

SHAW:

> Who told you to?

RENE:

> Nobody's got to tell me. I know my job.

SHAW:

> Rene, you were hired to do the shipping and I'm
> responsible for making decisions, is that correct?

RENE:

> Yeah maybe, but . . .

SHAW:

> Rene, is that understood?

RENE:

> Yeah.

SHAW:

> Good, now ship them all and the rest we'll send later.
> Oh, and Rene, no more sitting down on the job and
> that boy over there is using three staples on the boxes

RENE:

> So?

SHAW:

> So tell him to use two.

RENE:

Okay.

SHAW:

Rene.

RENE:

Yeah, yeah. Okay, okay. Hey, uh, Mike, how many times do I got to tell you? Use two staples on those boxes, not three, okay?

MIKE:

Two staples? But, uh, Rene?

RENE:

Use two staples, understand?

MIKE:

Uh, yeah.

RENE:

And, uh, Billy. Uh, no more sitting down on the job, okay?

BILLY gets up and SHAW exits.

RENE throws down his clipboard.

Moudez tête cawrey bloke, est-ti tabernack.

MIKE:

That new manager's a real winner, eh?

JACKY:

Yeah, grand prize, like a three week trip to Toronto.

MIKE:

Remember the one we used to have? The one there that had the nervous breakdown? He was always smiling.

JACKY:

> Started screaming in the can one morning and they had
> to carry him off.

MIKE:

> Always smiling.

JACKY:

> There he was, pants around his ankles screaming, "I
> can't take it no more. I can't take it no more." Ya
> shoulda been there, Gary. It was a gas.

MIKE:

> Always smiling. Like this.

> > *MIKE makes goofy face.*

JACKY:

> We were making bets on who was gonna crack up first.

MIKE:

> And Rene won and I betcha he beats this guy too.

JACKY:

> I dunno. This guy's pretty tough. I heard he's been to
> business school.

MIKE:

> Business school?

JACKY:

> Yeah, that's where guys like Shaw go and learn
> psychology. That's what they call it, Michael.
> Psychology.

MIKE:

> Yeah, I seen that one time.

JACKY:

> Yeah, they keep ya smiling while they work ya to
> death.

MIKE:

They must think we're awful dumb.

JACKY:

In your case, they're right.

He picks up a dress.

Look at this shit. They must be unloading this stuff in Ontario, man. Nobody in Montreal is gonna wear it.

RENE picks up a box from the cart and it falls apart. Dresses drop on the floor.

RENE:

Alright, pick it up. Get those dresses off the floor, Mike.

MIKE:

Not my fault, Rene. Two staples just don't hold those boxes together.

RENE:

So use three, you dummy.

MIKE:

Three?

RENE:

Yeah, one, two, three.

MIKE:

Yeah, but you said two and Shaw said that . . .

RENE:

Look, never mind what he said. Just use two staples when Shaw is around and three staples when he's not, understand? Do I have to tell you everything?

MIKE:
>Okay, three staples, one, two, three.

RENE:
>Alright, that cart's full. Bring it downstairs.

JACKY:
>Right.

RENE:
>Now, Thompson. No fucking around.

JACKY:
>Hey, man. Don't yell.

RENE:
>So don't get me mad and I don't yell, okay?

JACKY:
>Okay, fuck.

>*He stops.*

>Hey, Rene. We got the afternoon off, eh?

RENE:
>How should I know. Ask Shaw.

GARY:
>Hey, we always get the afternoon off.

RENE:
>Who says?

GARY:
>I'm asking you the question.

RENE:
>Boyce, if you don't like it here, leave it, okay?
>Understand? Got the message? Now, all of you move.
>Va-t-en! Get some fresh air.

MIKE, GARY, and JACKY exit with the cart.

RENE:

    Punks.

BILLY:

    They're pretty difficult, alright.

RENE:

    Punks, Billy. All we get now is punks.

BILLY:

    Do you want these copies?

RENE:

    Eh? Yeah . . . I used to have this shipping room running like a new machine, remember, Billy?

BILLY:

    Yeah.

RENE:

    No trouble, no fuss, 'cause everybody did their job and knew their place, but now . . . In the last five years, the kids been getting more and more like that Gary Boyce. Shit disturbers. They all got that look in their eye. Know what I mean? Like they don't give a damn.

BILLY:

    Well, times has changed, I guess.

RENE:

    Yeah, they're spoiled and they're smart. They're too smart. They don't obey the rules. You know what I mean?

BILLY:

    Yeah. Here's the 1807 invoices.

RENE:

> Thanks.

BILLY:

> Have we got the afternoon off?

RENE:

> No.

BILLY:

> Thought so.

RENE:

> Two big orders came in on urgent request. They're for Eaton's so we can't fuck around.

BILLY:

> The boys are tired. They aren't gonna like it.

RENE:

> Who cares if they don't like it. Do you think I like it? Eaton's tells Shaw. Shaw tells me and we do it. That's all.

BILLY:

> Yeah, I know.

RENE:

> Sure, you know and I know and the whole fuckin' world knows. You wanna be the foreman for awhile, Billy? You wanna know the real taste of shit?

BILLY:

> I understand.

RENE:

> Sure you understand.

BILLY:

> Take it easy.

RENE:

Yeah, take it easy. Come on, Billy. You know the game.

BILLY:

New manager's a real pain in the ass, eh?

RENE:

The new ones always are, but this is the worst. Tabernack.

BILLY:

You got an angle on him yet?

RENE:

I think so, but he's tricky, very tricky . . . I've got to keep these punks under control . . . Will you speak to them for me, Billy?

BILLY:

Uh, okay.

RENE:

I mean, they'll listen to you.

BILLY:

Yeah, sure. Okay, I'll see what I can do.

RENE:

I mean, we got no choice.

BILLY:

Yeah. Here's the 1050's.

RENE:

Thanks . . . Ah, shit . . . Uh, Billy, you know Shaw don't like anybody sitting down on the job, eh?

BILLY:

Yeah, but I work better sitting down.

RENE:

    I can't help that.

BILLY:

    My legs are bad this week, I . . .

RENE:

    Listen, Shaw already told me he wants a younger guy
    for your job and if he sees you sitting down . . .

BILLY:

    But Rene . . .

RENE:

    It's not me, Billy.

BILLY:

    Can't you talk to him?

RENE:

    No, I can't talk to him. He's out to get me too.
    Understand? Now, either you stand up or you go.
    That's all.

        BILLY gets up from his stool. The guys enter.
        JACKY is pushing the car with MIKE and
        GARY standing on it.

JACKY:

    Superior Dress Express.

RENE:

    Quit fucking around with those carts, Thompson.

JACKY: *making a Nazi salute*
    Ja-wohl.

RENE: *to GARY, fiddling with the cart*
    You think it's gonna be alright there? . . .

47

JACKY:
>Check it out, Billy.

>*He shows him another bottle, which is already open.*

BILLY:
>Jesus, another one.

MIKE:
>Yeah, we got this one from Finklestein.

JACKY:
>Yeah, I always give him extra dresses. Here.

>*He hands him over the bottle.*

BILLY:
>Put it away. Later.

RENE: *coming over*
>Okay, when you guys are finished with those orders start pulling down the 1050's from the racks. Mr. Jerome and Shaw will be around later with the Christmas bonuses.

GARY:
>Tell them we ain't working this afternoon.

>*RENE looks back at GARY, then exits.*

JACKY: *taking off his work apron*
>Fuck this shit, man. It's showtime.

>*He combs his hair and heads for the stairs.*

>You guys want any sandwiches?

RENE: *opening his office door*
>Mike.

He sees JACKY exiting.

Where you going?

JACKY:
　To the can.

RENE:
　Use your own can.

JACKY:
　It's broken.

RENE:
　Well, piss out the window. Mike, get me that pad off
　my desk. Hurry up.

　　　MIKE runs over and gets pad and throws it to
　　　RENE.

　Get back to work, Thompson. If I see you up here,
　you're fired.

　　　JACKY starts back towards the packing table.
　　　As RENE exits, he starts back up the stairs again.

JACKY:
　Fuck him, I'll go piss out their window.

　　　He exits out the office door.

MIKE: *laughing*
　That Jacky's too much, eh?

GARY:
　Yeah, thinks this is a Charlie Chaplin movie.

MIKE:
　Yeah, that Jacky's alright. He don't care about
　bosses. He don't care about nothing. Ya know, he's
　kind of a legend down in the Point too.

49

GARY:

>Yeah, I know.

MIKE:

>Yeah. Hey, first time I seen Jacky, man, he's eight years old, dancing up top a telephone pole. Yeah, a telephone pole right there on Wellington Street and me and a gang of guys standing there looking at all this and thinking, shit, he's crazy, and the cars stopped on the street and the cops chased him down, and well, it was beautiful, man. I was there and people still talk about it.

GARY:

>Yeah, I heard that story.

MIKE:

>Yeah, he's too much sometimes and other times . . .

>*He shakes his head.*

GARY:

>Yeah, but what's a nice guy like him doing in a place like this?

MIKE:

>Eh? . . . Gotta make a living, I guess.

GARY: *taking a slug from his bottle*

>Yeah, even legends gotta make a living, eh?

MIKE:

>Eh?

GARY:

>I said, even . . . Hey, Mike, tell me, are you really stupid or do you just act stupid?

MIKE:

>What?

GARY:

Are you really this stupid?

MIKE:

Hey, Gary. Hey, Billy.

GARY:

Come on, true confessions, Mike?

MIKE:

Hey. Uh, fuck. Why should I get smart, eh? . . . Hey, Gary. You're putting me on. You're getting drunk.

GARY:

I'm trying my best.

MIKE:

Yeah.

He takes a slug from GARY's bottle.

Me, I'm going to a party tonight.

JACKY: *from the office door at the top of the stairs*
Hey, Gary. Catch.

He throws down some sandwiches.

Come on, Mike. It's too much, man.

MIKE:

Hey, alright.

MIKE exits with JACKY.

BILLY:

Hey, you guys. Jesus, Mary and Joseph, we'll never get this done.

GARY:

Wanna sandwich, Billy?

BILLY:
    Eh?

GARY:
    Sandwich.

BILLY:
    Uh, yeah. Okay.

GARY: *handing him his bottle*
    Here, wash it down.

BILLY:
    No.

GARY:
    Go ahead.

BILLY:
    Aw, alright.

    He takes a big guzzle from the bottle.

GARY:
    Wow! You are Irish, eh?

BILLY:
    My father was.

GARY:
    Yeah. Well, we had this old Irish lady living upstairs
    from us in the Point when I was a kid. Mrs. Collins,
    a real nice old lady, and everybody on the block
    loved her and she loved everybody, everybody except
    landlords, man did she hate landlords. And whenever
    old Giboux came around for the rent she'd go out on
    her front gallery and scream, "May the dogs piss on
    his grave." Didn't like him at all.

BILLY:
    Yeah, some of the old Irish are like that.

GARY:
> Yeah, far as she's concerned there's only two kinds of people . . . Good people and landlords. And she's right.

BILLY:
> Well, I dunno? I don't think there's good people or bad people. There's just people.

GARY:
> Bullshit.

BILLY:
> Depends on what you learned in life. It's not good or bad. It, uh, just happens.

GARY:
> It just happens. Fuck.

BILLY:
> I'll take another shot of that bottle.

GARY:
> Yeah, sure.

> *He passes it over.*

BILLY:
> It kinda wakes me up.

> *He takes a small gulp this time.*

> Ah, maybe I oughta put some on my leg, eh? Feels good on the inside anyhow.

> *He passes him back the bottle.*

GARY:
> Yeah.

BILLY:

So Shaw and Jerome are coming around with the Christmas bonuses. That's a new one.

GARY'

Yeah, guess Shaw wants to try out some of his psychology, eh?

BILLY:

Yeah, right . . . So you were out late last night, eh?

GARY:

Yeah, I got stoned with a guy I used to know.

BILLY:

Old friend of yours?

GARY:

Yeah, he's a mess now, man. A speed freak. Total self-destruct trip.

BILLY:

That's too bad.

GARY:

Yeah. So many of the guys I knew on the street are gone dead or crazy, man. There's no escape. This whole country is just one big factory, one big jail, Billy. There's nowhere to go.

BILLY:

Seems that way sometimes.

GARY:

Like they got it all set up. Either you're a good nigger or ya die. Know what I mean?

BILLY:

I never liked the word, "nigger." I always call them coloured people.

GARY:

Oh, yeah? What colour?

BILLY:

Okay, Gary.

GARY:

Black, yellow, white. We're all niggers down on Rockefeller's Plantation, man.

BILLY:

Never liked the word.

GARY:

Yeah, well, fuck. It's gonna take a revolution to get rid of it.

BILLY:

Yeah, well, could be. Where the hell are those guys? Hey, we better do these invoices, eh? Invoices.

GARY:

Eh? Okay, by name or number?

BILLY:

We'll do these ones by name.

JACKY and MIKE enter.

JACKY:

Wow! It's a real joy mob in there.

MIKE:

Yeah. Wow! Got some more sandwiches.

He puts them on the table.

JACKY:
>
> People all letting loose. And Rene's there in the corner talking to Shaw and Jerome, the big boss, is there. A real dude. Got a hug from Judy and a little squeeze too.

MIKE:
>
> Yeah, and a slap in the face.

JACKY:
>
> She missed.

BILLY:
>
> Rene's talking to Shaw, eh?

JACKY:
>
> Yeah, looked right disturbed too. What's happening?

BILLY:
>
> I dunno.

JACKY:
>
> What's happening, Billy?

BILLY:
>
> Well . . . Rene's trying to get Shaw to give us the afternoon off.

JACKY:
>
> Hey, what?

BILLY:
>
> We don't have the afternoon off.

JACKY:
>
> Hey, fuck, what's the story?

BILLY:
>
> Look, a big order came in from Eaton's this morning and . . .

JACKY:

> So let them wait.

MIKE:

> Yeah, let them wait.

BILLY:

> We can't. It's Eaton's.

JACKY:

> Why not?

MIKE:

> Yeah, why not?

BILLY:

> Look, we'll get time and a half.

JACKY:

> Big fuckin' deal. It goes off in taxes.

MIKE:

> Yeah, taxes. And I gotta meet my girl.

BILLY:

> Well, Rene don't like it either, ya know.

JACKY:

> Fuck, I don't wanna work.

> *He punches a box.*

GARY:

> So, don't work . . . Tell Rene we're gonna walk off.
> How about that? Eh?

JACKY:

> Walk out?

GARY:

> Yeah.

BILLY:
    Forget it.

BILLY:
    Rene won't back us.

GARY:
    Ya told me he backed you guys once before.

JACKY:
    Yeah, but not this time.

GARY:
    Why not?

BILLY:
    Because Rene finally got that raise they promised him last year.

JACKY:
    Yeah, so he won't back us now and if we walk out, they'll just wave goodbye and bring in those goofs from the stock room to do our work. They got us fucked, Gary.

GARY:
    No wonder. You make it so easy for them. Billy, why don't you talk to Rene?

BILLY:
    I already did.

GARY:
    Look, we can make it so he has to back us.

BILLY:
    Forget it.

GARY:
    Fuck, it won't hurt to fight back.

BILLY:
 It's the wrong time, Gary. We're bound to lose.

GARY:
 Well, I ain't working this afternoon. How about you,
 Jacky?

JACKY:
 Been through this movie too many times, Gary.

GARY:
 Mike?

MIKE:
 I dunno.

GARY:
 Real hard rocks, eh? Big tough guys from the big
 tough Point, eh?

JACKY:
 Fuck off.

MIKE:
 Yeah, what the hell. Make some extra money, I guess.

JACKY:
 Ah, ya suck.

MIKE:
 Hey, what's with you?

JACKY:
 Suck, suck, suck.

MIKE:
 Oh, yeah? You get on my nerves, man.

JACKY: *grabbing MIKE by the shirt*
 Yeah. Oh, yeah?

MIKE:
>Uh, don't he get on your nerves, Gary?

JACKY:
>Fuck him and fuck you, man. Soon as I got my bike, I'm gone, man. Boom out of this fuckin' hole forever.

GARY:
>Where to, hard rock?

JACKY:
>Don't care, man. Just as long as I'm moving.

GARY:
>Round and round in circles like a squirrel in a cage.

JACKY:
>So what's it to you?

GARY:
>I've been there and back, that's all.

JACKY:
>Big shot, eh?

GARY:
>Toronto, Frisco, Vancouver, man. They're all the same and there's nowhere to go and nothing to do but go down dying right here, man.

JACKY:
>Yeah, well that's your head. Not my head, man. You're just talking about yourself.

GARY:
>Talk, talk, talk. Jail talk, beer talk, nigger talk. Pissing your life away.

JACKY:
>Don't get too loose, Gary.

GARY:
> Forget it. I got it, man.

JACKY:
> Listen, man . . .

> *JEROME, SHAW and RENE enter from the*
> *office. The guys get back to work. BILLY gets*
> *up from his stool.*

JEROME: *laughing and talking to SHAW*
> Oh, really? Everytime?

SHAW:
> Never fails. She thinks it's cute.

JEROME:
> You're not serious. Well, next time ask the girl how
> it's done. Har, har, har. Well . . . Hello . . . Uh . . .
> Hello . . . Richard, do we have the, uh . . .

> *RENE hands SHAW an envelope and he hands it*
> *to JEROME.*

SHAW:
> Yes, sir.

JEROME:
> Harry, Richard. Call me Harry.

> *He hands MIKE the envelope.*

> Uh, Merry Christmas. Uh . . .

RENE:
> Mike.

SHAW:
> Mike.

JEROME: *shaking MIKE's hand*
Mike.

MIKE:
You too, Harry. And hey . . . You too, Richard. Or
do they call ya Rick, eh? Call ya Rick?

JEROME: *laughs*
Well, yes . . . And there we . . .

JACKY:
John. The name's John, Harry.

JEROME:
Yes. Well, John . . . Merry Christmas, John.

*He hands JACKY an envelope and shakes his
hand.*

JACKY:
Yeah. Nice tan you got there. Just back from Florida?

JEROME:
Uh, Bermuda actually. Very nice down there, you
know. But well . . . What's Christmas without a little
snow, eh? Ha, ha.

MIKE:
Ha, ha, ha. A little snow.

JACKY:
Yeah. Covers up the ground.

*JEROME heads toward GARY who exits out
the back without shaking his hand.*

JEROME:
Who? What? Who's that? . . .

RENE:
Uh, Mr. Jerome, this is Bill. You know, Bill Reilly.

62

JEROME:
> Bill? . . . Oh yes, Bill Reilly. Of course. Well . . .
> You've been with us some time, haven't you?

BILLY:
> Yeah.

JEROME:
> Well . . . Merry Christmas, Bill.

> *He shakes his hand and hands BILLY an envelope.*

BILLY:
> Thank you.

JEROME:
> No, thank *you*. Well, is that everyone?

SHAW:
> Yes. And now we'll go cheer up the boys in the stock
> room, shall we?

JEROME:
> Good. Tell me, is old Nathan still there?

SHAW:
> Yes, I believe so.

JEROME:
> You know, Nathan worked for my father too.

SHAW:
> Oh, really? Excuse me for just one moment, Harry.

> *To RENE.*

> That boy who just left, get rid of him. I don't like his
> attitude.

RENE:
> But we need him for the Eaton's order . . .

SHAW:
> So punch his card after the order is complete.

> *He hands RENE GARY's envelope.*

RENE:
> But . . .

SHAW:
> Rene . . . Well, Harry, I was telling you about this girl . . .

JEROME:
> Oh yes, go on. She sounds real kinky.

SHAW:
> Yes. So really, there she was, a real swinger and . . .

> *SHAW and JEROME exit. RENE hands BILLY GARY's envelope, then exits after the others.*

MIKE:
> Fifty beans.

BILLY:
> The same as last year.

JACKY: *mimicking JEROME*
> Is old Nathan still working here? Yeah, sure. Over there hanging by his thumbs. Whip, whip, whip.

> *GARY enters.*

> Five gets you ten, you're out of a job, man.

BILLY: *handing GARY his envelope*
> Here's yours.

GARY:
> Oh, happy day.

MIKE:

Fifty beans, eh?

GARY:

Yeah, now I can go weigh myself five hundred times.

JACKY:

Hey, Shaw wasn't too pleased there with the grand exit.

MIKE:

Said he didn't like your altitude.

GARY:

Fuck him.

JACKY:

It looked like you left like that on purpose.

GARY:

I did.

JACKY:

Why?

GARY:

Why not? I'm a free man.

JACKY:

No, Gary. Tell me why?

GARY:

Look, I don't like the man. I don't like his style and I don't wanna shake his hand, okay?

JACKY:

I shook his hand. We all shook his hand. Something wrong with us?

GARY:

Don't start again.

JACKY:
>   There's something wrong with us, eh?

GARY:
>   Fuck right off!

JACKY:
>   Hey, man. Hey, come on. I'm ready.

GARY:
>   Aw, fuck off.

>   *JACKY swings on GARY and MIKE and BILLY break it up.*

BILLY:
>   Go on, go on. Take a walk, Jacky. Go with him, Mike.

JACKY:
>   Fuckin' goof.

BILLY:
>   Go with him, Mike.

JACKY:
>   You're not the only one who's been around, man.

BILLY:
>   Go with him, Mike. Go on, take a walk.

>   *JACKY and MIKE exit.*

BILLY:
>   Jesus, what . . . Why did ya do that?

GARY:
>   Ah.

BILLY:
>   Jacky's got a bad temper.

GARY:

It's all peanut butter, Billy.

BILLY:

Yeah, eh?

GARY:

Yeah, it's sticky, it's gooey and it spreads.

BILLY:

Yeah, well don't fool around with Jacky like that.

GARY:

Yeah, okay. You're right . . . But . . . Shaking Jerome's
hand . . . I mean, I'm not saying I'm better than you
guys. But I just can't stand being treated like that.

BILLY:

So what's wrong with Jerome?

GARY:

Nothing's wrong with Jerome, okay? He was born
where he was and I was born where I was, but . . .
Sometimes I wish everything I hate in life had just
one face.

BILLY:

Well, maybe Rene'll stick up for ya.

GARY:

Rene only sticks up for himself. Number one. Can't
be a foreman and a nice guy, eh?

BILLY:

Okay, okay. Let's get some work done. We got a long
day.

GARY:

Not me, I'm fired.

He takes a slug from his drink.

BILLY:

> You're not gonna screw up on us, are ya, Gary? I
> mean . . .

GARY:

> Don't worry.

BILLY:

> I mean, we don't wanna lose our jobs.

GARY:

> Don't worry, I'll leave at lunchtime.

> *JACKY and MIKE enter.*

MIKE: *to JACKY*

> Okay? Forget it.

GARY: *holding out his bottle to JACKY*

> Hey, man. Maybe I deserved a punch in the head, eh?

JACKY:

> Fuck.

GARY:

> Come on, have a drink.

JACKY:

> Watch yourself, Gary.

GARY:

> I'll watch myself. Look, I'm watching myself. Okay?

> *He stares down at his balls.*

MIKE: *laughing*

> Hey.

> *JACKY hesitates, then takes the bottle.*

JACKY:

Aw, fuck. It's been a long week.

MIKE:

Hey, see old Jacky there doing the Peanuts Boucher, eh? Pow, pow, pow.

JACKY:

Yeah, did I hurt ya, man?

GARY:

Naw, you're a bad shot when you're drinking, pal. Hey, here's to the last of the true cowboys of Point Saint Charles.

JACKY:

Yeah, I'll drink to that. Hey, later we'll hit the tavern for lunch, right?

GARY:

Sounds like a stupendous idea.

MIKE:

Stupendous.

JACKY:

Gary's getting drunk.

GARY:

Yeah, I understand it, but can't stand it.

JACKY:

He is getting drunk.

MIKE:

Hey.

MIKE, GARY
AND JACKY: *altogether*
> We don't care for all the rest of Canada.
> All the rest of Canada.
> All the rest of Canada.
> We don't care for all the rest of Canada.
> We're from Point Saint Charles. Hey.

> *Repeat.*

JACKY: *throwing an empty bottle at the garbage can*
> He shoots . . . He shoots, he scores.

MIKE
AND GARY:
> YAAAH!

BILLY:
> Hey, pipe down.

JACKY:
> Woo. Yeah, the old school song.

MIKE:
> Yeah. We lost all the games, but we won all the fights.

BILLY:
> Hey, we got work to do, you guys.

> *GARY starts the song and JACKY and MIKE join in.*

GARY, JACKY
AND MIKE: *altogether*
> One of these days I'm gonna wake up crazy,
> Shoot the wife and sell the babies.

> Come on boys, have a drink on me.

> *JEROME, SHAW and RENE enter.*

Have a drink, have a drink, have a drink on me,
Everybody here have a drink on me.

SHAW:

What's this?

The guys scatter, except for GARY.

RENE:

What the hell are you doing?

GARY: *still sitting on the packing table with a bottle*
I'm singing your song, Rene.

JEROME:

What's he doing?

SHAW:

Just a trouble maker, Harry.

RENE:

Get up.

JEROME:

What's he doing?

GARY:

I'm contemplating. I'm an orphan and I'm contemplating suicide.

SHAW:

He's drunk.

RENE:

You're drunk.

GARY:

I'm drunk. Hey, Harry. What's Christmas without a little snow, eh? Bermuda, Bermuda.

RENE:
> Hey, smarten up.

GARY:
> Tell me, Rene. Am I fired?

SHAW:
> He's fired.

RENE:
> You're fired.

GARY:
> I'm fired. Gosh, shucks, holy cow. Tell me it isn't true? It isn't true.

JEROME:
> What is this? What is this?

SHAW:
> Nothing, Harry. Just a trouble maker. Come this way.

JEROME:
> No, Richard, if there's trouble, I like to know about it. Well, what's the problem?

GARY:
> Bermuda, Bermuda.

JEROME:
> Well, come on, Billy? Tell me what's the problem?

BILLY:
> Well, uh, we have to work this afternoon.

JEROME:
> And?

BILLY:
> And up to now we've always had the afternoon off on Christmas Eve.

JEROME:
> Is that so?

SHAW:
> Well, there's no fixed rule, Harry, but uh . . .

JEROME:
> Then why the exception? Why all this trouble?

SHAW:
> A special order in from Eaton's, Harry.

JEROME:
> So. They can wait, can't they?

SHAW:
> It's Eaton's, Harry.

JEROME:
> I don't care who it is.

SHAW:
> But . . .

JEROME:
> And I don't care to discuss it. Does Eaton's tell you what to do, Richard? Don't we have our own schedule?

SHAW:
> Well, yes, of course but . . .

JEROME:
> So let Eaton's wait and give the boys the afternoon off, for God's sake. You're off at lunch, boys. Merry Christmas.

> > *He shakes hands with GARY, catching him by surprise.*

MIKE
AND JACKY:
Same to you.

JEROME, SHAW and RENE exit.

JACKY:
Love it, love it. Hey, did you see old Shaw cringing
Grovel, grovel, grovel, when Jerome gave him the
word, eh? And Gary here. You're too much, man.
I love ya.

GARY:
Yeah, too much.

MIKE:
Hey, Bermuda, Bermuda.

JACKY:
You oughta talk to Jerome, Gary. He's good people.
Might get your job back.

GARY:
Good guys, bad guys. Aw, don't bother me right now.

JACKY:
He understands it, but he can't stand it.

MIKE:
Wants to contemplate.

GARY:
Yeah, lemme contemplate.

BILLY:
Come on. Let's get these orders done.

JACKY:
Hey, it's too much, eh, Billy?

BILLY:
>Nice surprise.

JACKY:
>Did ya see his face, eh? Fuck, that was good.

MIKE: *getting back to work*
>Hey.

>*He starts to sing and JACKY joins in.*

JACKY
AND MIKE:
>Born in a garbage can in Saint Henri,
>Lost his mother in the A&P,
>Killed his father with a can of beans,
>And got himself a dose when he was only three.
>
>Gary, Gary Crockett,
>King of the Wild Frontier.

>*There is no response from GARY who is still
>sitting with a bottle in his hand.*

MIKE:
>Hey, you remember Danny O'Connor?

JACKY:
>Yeah, what about him?

MIKE:
>Man, he was a tough guy, eh?

JACKY:
>Not so tough.

MIKE:
>Oh, yeah. He shot a cop once.

JACKY:
>Yeah, but he only shot him in the foot.

MIKE:
Well, nobody's perfect.

RENE enters.

JACKY:
Hey, Rene.

RENE pushes him out of the way.

RENE:
The stool, Billy, the stool.

BILLY gets up.

What the hell you doing here, Boyce?

GARY:
Who me? I'm relaxing.

RENE:
You're fired, so get the fuck outta here.

GARY:
No.

RENE:
Think I'm kidding?

GARY:
Go ahead and try it.

RENE:
Think I'm afraid?

GARY:
Try it.

RENE:
Mike, go punch his card. And you, smart guy, stay out of this. Understand?

76

MIKE exits.

RENE:

Hey, you guys. I want to talk to you.

JACKY:

Yeah?

RENE:

Yeah, we're working this afternoon.

JACKY:

No fuckin' way.

BILLY:

Who says?

RENE:

Shaw.

BILLY:

That figures.

JACKY:

Hey Rene, but Jerome's the owner and he said . . .

RENE:

Listen, Jerome don't know nothing about what it takes to make him money and it's money that keeps him happy and us with the jobs, so we're working this afternoon. That's all.

MIKE enters.

JACKY:

Fuck.

MIKE:

Hey, what's happening?

RENE:

    You know what to do if you don't like it.

JACKY:

    Lump it, right?

RENE:

    Right.

MIKE:

    Hey, Jacky, Rene. What's happening?

BILLY:

    It's impossible, Rene. The boys are half drunk.

RENE:

    Okay, okay. I know you guys been drinking. Look,
    I'll get Irving downstairs to have the old man bring up
    some coffee and you can have an hour and a half for
    lunch. How's that?

JACKY:

    Fuck you.

RENE:

    Oh and fuck you too. Now that's the way it is. Now
    let's get going and get this over with. And you, smart
    guy, go down the back and start pulling those 1050's.
    Now!

    JACKY doesn't move.

GARY: *with a bottle, singing*
    One of these days gonna wake up crazy,
    Shoot the wife and sell the babies.

RENE:

    Shut up, Boyce. Just shut up.

    He goes to the telephone.

Hello, Irving? Yeah, yeah. Never mind the Christmas jokes. So listen, send up some coffee and doughnuts for the boys. Yeah, some doughnuts and two regular, one without sugar and a Coke. Hey Mike, you wanna Coke?

BILLY is putting on his boots and coat.

Hey Billy, where the hell you going?

BILLY:
Home.

RENE:
Hang on, Irving. Ah, come on.

MIKE:
Hey, are we getting off early?

BILLY:
I've had enough, Rene.

RENE:
Billy.

BILLY:
It's all yours now, Rene.

RENE:
Billy, it's just another afternoon like all the others.

JACKY: *joining BILLY*
Yeah, only we ain't gonna be there.

BILLY:
Look, Rene.

RENE:
This is crazy, Billy.

BILLY:
I can't last much longer anyway.

RENE:
These punks don't give a damn, Billy. But you got a family. Hey.

GARY:
Trouble with you is you think you got something to lose.

RENE:
Shut up.

GARY:
Temper, temper.

BILLY:
Well, what's the use?

JACKY: *putting on his jacket.*
Yeah, come on, Mike. You coming, Gary?

GARY:
No.

JACKY:
No?

GARY:
It's cold outside. I'm staying here.

JACKY:
What's that?

GARY:
Look, if you guys leave right now, you'll just make things easier for Shaw. Smart thing to do is just sit here and let them worry for a change. I'm serious.

JACKY:

　　You mean, stick and stay?

GARY:

　　Yeah.

JACKY:

　　Like a demonstration or something?

GARY:

　　Yeah, just sit here and say no, we ain't working and
　　no, we ain't moving. No.

JACKY:

　　Hey, yeah. Why not? Sounds like a gas.

GARY:

　　Sure, why not? Right, Billy?

BILLY:

　　I'm going.

GARY:

　　Billy, we got a choice.

BILLY:

　　Some choice.

GARY:

　　Yeah, but at least they'll remember us, Billy. Look,
　　if you walk out that door, you're gone. That's all.
　　Just another old man walking down the street.
　　Gone. Help us, Billy. Help yourself.

JACKY:

　　Yeah, Billy.

RENE:

　　This is all a joke.

BILLY: *taking off his coat.*
Aw, what the hell.

GARY:
That's my man.

He hugs BILLY.

MIKE:
We're not getting off early?

GARY:
Rene, we're on strike.

RENE:
It is a joke.

GARY:
Watch us.

RENE:
Jacky, you in on this crazy thing?

JACKY:
Yeah.

RENE:
Mike?

MIKE:
Huh?

JACKY:
Yeah, he's in on it too. Mike, we're on strike.

MIKE:
On strike?

RENE:
And I'm the bad guy, eh?

BILLY:
> You don't have to be.

JACKY:
> Yeah, Rene. Come on. Have a drink. Forget it. It's game over.

MIKE:
> On strike.

RENE:
> Look, all I gotta do is tell Shaw what you doing and he'll have another crew working in here in five minutes.

GARY:
> Nobody works in here, understand?

RENE:
> So then they call in the cops.

GARY:
> Yeah, do that and we'll be on every front page in the fuckin' country.

JACKY:
> Yeah, Rene. What the fuck. Why don't you join us?

RENE:
> Three punks and one crazy old man. Okay, I've backed you guys before? I've done you favours?

JACKY:
> Yeah, so?

RENE:
> Okay, the union boss is at the office party. Why don't you talk to him?

JACKY:
> What for?

RENE:

What do you mean, what for? That's why you pay
union dues so you can talk to someone about your
troubles.

GARY:

How about that?

MIKE:

I always thought union dues was some kind of taxes.

JACKY:

No tricks?

RENE:

Tricks? Hey, I'm in this mess too, eh? I'm the one
that gets the shit from them. Well, so you wanna
talk to him?

BILLY:

Sure, won't hurt to try, I guess.

GARY:

Yeah, let's make this strike official.

JACKY:

Alright.

MIKE:

Hey, Rene. Irving's still on the phone.

RENE:

Tabernack.

He rushes over and picks up the telephone.

Hello, Irving? Yeah, sorry. No, cancelling the order.
Sorry. What? Fuck you too. Mange lamarde. Tabernack.

*He slams down the telephone and exits to the
office.*

GARY: *pulling out a stool*
Have a seat, Billy. Feels good, eh?

JACKY:
Yeah, this is gonna be fun. How come we never done this before?

MIKE:
So we're on strike, eh? Just like on the TV news?

GARY:
Right.

MIKE:
Wow!

JACKY:
So here we are telling those smucks what to do. I like it, I like it.

GARY:
Yeah, it's a new game now with new rules.

JACKY:
I'll drink to that.

MIKE: *making a Panther salute*
Hey, right on!

JACKY:
You really do watch the TV news, eh?

MIKE:
Yeah, sure. Yeah and last week I seen these guys on strike and they were all carrying signs and . . . Hey, we gotta make some signs.

He goes and gets some cardboard.

JACKY: *shaking his head*
Sleeping Beauty.

BILLY:
>No rough stuff, eh?

GARY:
>If they get rough, we get tough.

BILLY:
>Well, I'll just leave if you do.

JACKY:
>Relax, Billy. We're gonna have a good time.

BILLY:
>Yeah.

GARY:
>Hey. Come on, man. Now's our chance.

>*RENE enters with the UNION BOSS.*

UNION BOSS: *drink in one hand, sandwich in the other*
>Where? The shipping room? I thought you said the
>stock room. Down there? Hi, hello. So how's every-
>thing? Okay? Not too bad, not too good? Comme ci,
>comme ça? Har, har, har.

>*There is no response.*

>Well . . . So Rene here tells me you guys got a
>grievance? Speak up and let's see what we can do
>about it?

JACKY:
>Go on, Billy.

BILLY:
>Well, uh . . . Well, I guess we feel we're being over-
>worked.

UNION BOSS:
>Overworked, eh? Lots of rush orders this season?

BILLY:
>   Yes.

UNION BOSS:
>   Lots of overtime, eh?

BILLY:
>   We're working a sixty-hour week.

UNION BOSS:
>   Hey, that's tough. That's really tough. Are you being paid time and a half?

BILLY:
>   Well, yeah.

UNION BOSS:
>   They don't have you working Saturdays, do they?

BILLY:
>   Well, they tried.

UNION BOSS:
>   But you didn't?

BILLY:
>   No.

UNION BOSS:
>   Good for you. Well . . . That's it?

BILLY:
>   Uh, I guess so.

UNION BOSS:
>   Well, in that case it seems the company is within the law as far as our contract is concerned. So really you boys only have general grievances. That is to say that Jerome is within his legal rights as far as our contract is concerned.

MIKE:
>What's he talking about?

BILLY:
>I don't know. I haven't seen the contract.

UNION BOSS:
>I mean, there's nothing going on like short pay or hiring non-union labour is there?

BILLY:
>No. But the hours . . . The hours are too long during the rush season and during the slack season they lay us off. We either work too hard or too little.

UNION BOSS:
>Yeah, I know it's a tough industry and believe me, I know how hard it can get . . . And we're working on the difficult problem of the hours . . . But meanwhile . . . .C'est la vie, eh? . . . I mean, when the work is there, it's there. And when it's not, it's not.

JACKY:
>Oh, fuck.

MIKE:
>Is he gonna help us?

UNION BOSS:
>Look, usually in cases like this we ask the members to mail a list of their grievances to the Union headquarters where the list is read, duly considered by a special committee and filed for further use by our committee of inspectors.

GARY: *getting up with a piece of paper*
>Yeah, sure. Uh, your list, uh, will be read, uh, duly considered and, uh, filed for further use by our, uh, inspectors.

He deliberately drops the paper into a waste-paper basket.

UNION BOSS:
No, but seriously. I can understand why you boys are upset, but these things do happen, and we're a big international organization dedicated to the well-being of all of our workers, not just some of them, and . . .

GARY:
Money talks and bullshit walks.

UNION BOSS:
And I know Jerome. I personally know him and up to now we've had no serious problems with him . . . So I think, considering the total situation, and realizing how complicated the situation has become, that perhaps tentatively . . .

JACKY:
Duh? I had one, but the wheels fell off.

UNION BOSS:
What?

JACKY:
What?

UNION BOSS:
What?

JACKY:
Duh, what?

UNION BOSS:
As I was saying . . .

GARY:
Hey, Fats.

UNION BOSS:
> Tentatively as a prerequisite . . .

GARY:
> Hey, Fats.

UNION BOSS:
> What?

GARY:
> Hey. We're not interested in hearing how well your business is doing. We just wanna know if you'll stand by us?

UNION BOSS:
> For what?

GARY:
> For taking the afternoon off.

MIKE:
> We're going on strike. You wanna join us?

UNION BOSS:
> On strike? Get serious. Hey, Rene.

JACKY:
> We're doing it.

UNION BOSS:
> You got no authority.

GARY:
> We don't need it.

UNION BOSS:
> You'll get no support from us.

GARY:
> We don't want it. If we do it ourselves, we don't need you, eh?

UNION BOSS:
>It's stupid. Hey, you guys are all drunk.

GARY:
>Drunk or sober, we got your number.

UNION BOSS:
>Better talk to these guys, Rene.

JACKY: *stopping the UNION BOSS*
>Hey, man. Those shoes. Where'd you get those groovy shoes? I really like those shoes.

UNION BOSS:
>Out of the way.

JACKY:
>And that tie, man. I really dig that tie.

UNION BOSS:
>Hands off.

GARY:
>Hey. What's that on your nose? Something on your nose? Where you been putting your nose lately?

RENE:
>Alright, alright.

JACKY:
>Yeah. Nose.

>*He grabs his nose.*

UNION BOSS:
>Hey. Fuck off.

GARY: *pushing the UNION BOSS*
>Hey. Watch it.

JACKY: *pushing him too*
Yeah. Don't get pushy, man.

UNION BOSS:
Rene.

RENE:
Okay, okay. Enough.

JACKY:
Hit the road, toad. Get it out of here, Rene.

UNION BOSS:
I'll remember this.

GARY:
You do that.

RENE and the UNION BOSS exit together.

GARY and JACKY laugh and slap five.

GARY:
NEXT!

BILLY:
There's no need for that.

JACKY:
Yeah, Billy . . . But it's fun.

BILLY:
Some fun. We might have got somewhere with that guy.

GARY:
Uh, tentative, uh, total situation, and let me make this perfectly clear that, uh, the situation is total, and uh . . . Dork, dork, dork, dork . . .

JACKY:
Aw, come on, Billy. Loosen up.

BILLY:
Yeah, sure.

JACKY:
Yeah. So, what happens next?

GARY:
Well, and now the plot sickens as we move into the final round. Ladies and kind gentlemen . . .

BILLY:
He's drunk out of his head.

MIKE:
Hey.

Writing a sign.

Hey, here it comes.

He holds up the sign.

Hey, what do ya think?

JACKY: *reading*

We're so uptight,
We can't sleep nights.
So we went on strike
To get our rights.

Hey, fuck. He's a poet.

MIKE:
Yeah, I'm a fuckin' poet and I'm gonna put the sign right over here so when those TV cameras come in, they can get a good shot at it.

JACKY: *striking a pose using a bottle as a microphone*
Yeah, right. Lights, cameras, action! Good evening,
everybody out there in TV land and tonight on
F.U.C.K., we're proud to present live, a genuine strike
already in progress, and over here we have a genuine,
uh, picturesque example of, uh . . .

GARY:
Downtrodden worker type.

JACKY:
Yeah, right. Downtrodden worker type. Tough life,
eh?

GARY:
Yeah.

JACKY:
Speak into the mike, kid.

GARY: *striking a Shakespearian pose with one hand to his
forehead* My friends and fellow countrymen . . .
Foursooth, fivesooth, sixsooth, sevensooth . . .

JACKY:
Yes and . . .

GARY:
Metaphor, metafive, metasix.

JACKY:
Yes and moving right along . . .

He hands the microphone over to BILLY.

BILLY:
No comment.

JACKY:
No comment. Yes and . . .

MIKE:
>Hey, hey. Hi, Ma. It's me. I'm on strike. I'm not
>stupid. I'm just acting stupid.

JACKY:
>And moving right along . . .

GARY: *striking a soapbox pose*
>And now you see us here in a familiar situation going
>up and down the snakes and ladders, losing again and
>bound to lose, but in the grand tradition of those
>captains on their sinking ships, we say, "Fuck you.
>We have only begun to lose . . ."

MIKE
AND JACKY: *cheering*
>Yaah!

GARY:
>And tired of waiting for the mail and the promises
>and the heroes and the leaders, we're gonna do it
>ourselves and lose . . .

MIKE
AND JACKY: *cheering*
>Yaah!

GARY:
>And lose . . .

MIKE
AND JACKY: *cheering*
>Yaah!

GARY:
>And lose and lose and lose and keep on losing . . .

MIKE
AND JACKY: *cheering*
>Yaah!

GARY:
> Until overwhelmed by our defeats, we shall win.

MIKE
AND JACKY: *cheering*
> Yaaah!

GARY:
> When the ocean moves, everything moves.

> *They cheer.*

BILLY:
> Hey, you guys . . .

GARY:
> It's our choice and I promise, if selected to stay on my side, which is our side . . .

> *They cheer.*

> To fight for myself, for the people who work, the working people, the working class, for united we stand and divided they stand . . .

> *They cheer.*

BILLY:
> Hey.

GARY:
> And to further complicate this occasion I would further like to say . . .

JACKY:
> Put Shaw in a box and ship him to Chabougamou.

MIKE:
> Rivière du Loup.

GARY:

>Armpit, Ontario. Third class . . . And I will now call for further desolution on the question . . .

JACKY:

>Stupendous!

GARY:

>Tentative.

MIKE:

>Mozzarella!

JACKY:

>Mozzarella?

GARY:

>Is there life before death? Will Mohammed make it to the mountain? If I'm me, can you be you? Tell me it isn't true.

MIKE:

>It isn't true.

GARY:

>Thank you, thank you.

MIKE:

>Right on, right on, right on.

JACKY:

>Right off, right off . . . And now a word from our sponsors. Has your teenage son run away from home? Could it be your breath? Try whiskey. It's got possibilities . . . And now back to our strike and remember, you saw it first on F.U.C.K. . . .

GARY: *throwing dresses in the air*
>Hey, free dresses. Free dresses.

JACKY:
   Yes, it's share the wealth time and here we have . . .

MIKE: *throwing dresses in the air*
   Free dresses.

JACKY:
   Free beer and chicken. Share the wealth.

GARY:
   Free dresses.

MIKE:
   Hey, I want one for my granny in the Point. I'm
   serious.

JACKY:
   What size, my friend?

MIKE: *spreading his arms*
   What size is this?

JACKY:
   That? That's a tent.

GARY: *still throwing dresses up*
   Free dresses. Share the wealth.

   BILLY starts to leave.

GARY:
   Hey, Billy.

JACKY:
   Billy.

GARY:
   What the fuck ya doing?

BILLY:
   I'm leaving. You guys'll do alright.

GARY:

> We need ya. Ya can't go now.

JACKY:

> Who's gonna talk to Rene?

MIKE:

> Yeah.

BILLY:

> It's all getting too crazy.

JACKY:

> Aw, Billy. Have a drink. You'll feel better.

MIKE:

> Yeah.

BILLY:

> No, I better go.

JACKY:

> Come on, Billy.

MIKE:

> Come on.

BILLY:

> No, I mean it. Now leave me alone.

GARY:

> AW, FUCK!

> > *He bumps into a rack of dresses, grabs the rack
> > and knocks it over.*

> Aw, fuck! That's right. Give up.

JACKY:

> Hey, Gary.

GARY:
It's me that's trapped 'cause you goofs always give up.

JACKY:
Hey, man.

GARY:
Ya always give up.

JACKY:
Hey, man. Don't freak out.

GARY:
You old fart.

BILLY:
Gary, it's not . . . It's crazy . . .

GARY:
Yeah. Well, tell me where ya going, Billy, eh? Tell me that?

BILLY:
Gary.

JACKY:
If he wants to go, let him go, man.

GARY:
Fuck!

RENE and SHAW enter.

SHAW:
What is this?

MIKE: *ducking behind JACKY*
Oh no.

RENE:
Moudez Crist!

SHAW:

> Look at those dresses. What is this?

RENE:

> Alright, pick them up.

> > *GARY picks up some dresses and throws them in the air.*

> Jacky, Mike. Pick them up.

> > *MIKE starts picking them up, but JACKY stands on top of a dress and starts pulling at it.*

SHAW:

> He's standing on them.

> > *JACKY rips one and hands it to RENE.*

> Alright, that's it. Rene, punch their cards. They've had it. I want them all out of here in five minutes. Five minutes, Rene!

RENE: *picking up some dresses*
> Alright, alright.

SHAW:

> It's your responsibility, not mine. Remember that.

RENE:

> Okay, okay.

SHAW:

> I'm holding you responsible for all this.

RENE:

> Okay, I heard you alright!

SHAW:

> Five minutes, Rene.

He exits.

RENE:

Well, that's it. You bastards finally pushed it over on top of me.

BILLY:

Oh shit.

RENE:

It's all over now.

BILLY:

Rene. Come on, you guys. Let's clean up.

GARY: *holding up five fingers*
Five minutes, Rene.

RENE:

Smiling, eh, Gary? You like it, eh?

BILLY:

Never mind him, Rene.

RENE:

You like it, eh? Makes you feel like a big man?

BILLY:

Come on, Rene. We'll fix up the place. We don't want, uh . . .

RENE:

What are ya gonna do, Billy?

GARY:

Ya dumb fuckin' Pepsi.

BILLY:

Gary.

GARY:

> All this work for nothing, eh, Rene?

RENE:

> Punk. Stupid kid.

GARY:

> Thought you knew where it's at, but it's gone, eh, Rene?

BILLY:

> Gary.

RENE:

> What's your face gonna look like in ten years, eh?

GARY:

> Suck, suck. Sell your soul for a car and a TV set.

RENE:

> You'll be in the taverns with scabs on your nose.

BILLY:

> Rene, forget it.

GARY:

> Cheap, Rene. Dirt cheap and now they don't want you no more. Fini, finished, kaput. Off to the glue factory. Cheap, cheap, cheap.

RENE:

> You'll be there and you'll know it.

GARY:

> Cheap, cheap, cheep.

> > *RENE and GARY start to fight. They fall down fighting.*

BILLY:

> Jacky, get him off. Get him off.

JACKY:
Hey, Gary. Hey, man. Stop it. You're hitting the wrong people.

MIKE:
Rene.

Helping him up.

Hey, Billy. He's bleeding.

RENE looks at his hand. SHAW enters.

SHAW:
What? What is this? . . . I'm phoning the police.

He heads towards the telephone, but JACKY grabs him.

JACKY:
You ain't phoning anybody.

He punches SHAW.

Gonna knock your fuckin' teeth down your throat . . .

RENE:
Let him go, Jacky. Let him go.

SHAW breaks loose and runs up the stairs.

The guys throw dresses after him.

SHAW:
You saw that. I want witnesses. I want witnesses.

He ducks behind the office door and exits.

JACKY: *taking a deep breath*
Yeah, yeah, yeah.

He walks away from the stairs.

RENE:

Okay. Come on, you guys.

BILLY starts to pick up some of the dresses.

Don't worry about that now, Billy. You guys just better go before the cops get here, okay? Go on.

The guys start to get dressed to leave.

BILLY goes and gets the first aid kit.

BILLY:

Lemme look at your hand.

RENE:

Just a scratch.

BILLY starts taking things out of the kit and dressing the cut.

JACKY:

Hey, uh, Rene, uh, you want some help with the cops?

RENE:

No, it's uh, better you just go . . . Thanks.

JACKY:

Yeah, eh? Okay.

MIKE: *to JACKY*

Tell him we're going to the tavern.

JACKY:

Oh yeah. Hey, Rene. We're going to the tavern. Wanna join us?

RENE:

Maybe later.

JACKY:
>
> Yeah, okay. See ya, Rene. Salut.

MIKE:
>
> See ya, Rene. Come on, Gary.

GARY:
>
> Hey, uh, Rene?

RENE:
>
> What?

GARY:
>
> I, uh, bit drunk, uh, didn't mean to . . .

RENE:
>
> Eh?

GARY:
>
> I'm sorry.

RENE:
>
> I'm sorry for you too, kid.

> *JACKY, MIKE and GARY exit.*

BILLY:
>
> What about you?

RENE:
>
> Somebody's got to talk to the cops.

BILLY:
>
> No, I mean will they fire you too?

RENE:
>
> Not right away. Maybe a week, a month. Soon as they find a new guy. Younger guy.

BILLY:
>
> The bastards.

RENE: *shrugging*
> They just do what they got to do . . . Think he meant
> it, Billy?

BILLY:
> Who? Gary. When he said he was sorry.

RENE:
> Yeah.

BILLY:
> Sure. Why else would he say it?

RENE:
> Yeah, well . . .

> *Thinking.*

> Look at this mess. Look at it . . . Years I spent getting
> here, Billy. Years and years of going to work, going
> home, feeding the kids, going to sleep, going to work
> . . . Yes, boss. No, boss . . . All that time just for
> this?

BILLY:
> Well, I seen it coming.

RENE:
> That's right.

BILLY:
> Hold still.

RENE:
> That's right. I seen it coming too. I seen it coming a
> long time . . . It's crazy when you think of it. All the
> tricks and games we have to play just to make dresses
> for women to wear, eh?

BILLY:
> It's crazy alright.

107

RENE:

It's bad. It's bad the way we have to live when you
don't want to live this way. It's bad. It's bullshit
what I got to do just to work. To yell and scream and
tell you to sit up and sit down. It's bad.

BILLY:

Not your fault.

RENE:

It's everybody's fault. You make your bed and you
sleep in it.

BILLY:

Guess so.

RENE:

Why you smiling?

BILLY:

Oh, thinking about Jacky punching out Shaw.

RENE:

Yeah, that was nice to see, eh?

BILLY:

It's my one good memory of this place.

RENE:

Yeah, well . . . Some people only understand a punch
in the nose. It might make him more human, who
knows . . . And me, you know in a way I feel better.
It's gone, no more bullshit, because me, I can't take
it no more. Shaw, he thinks he can do it, but he
can't. People don't believe in nothing no more.
Nobody cares, nobody believes. Hey, ouch. Go easy
on that iodine, tabernack.

BILLY:

Sorry. Hold still.

RENE:

Okay . . . Look at this mess . . . A Depression coming too, I think. Think there's gonna be another Depression, Billy?

BILLY:

Sure looks that way.

RENE:

And Québec now, they talk of revolution.

BILLY:

Well, never can tell. I can't see young guys like Jacky and Gary standing in soup lines like I did, can you?

RENE:

Aw, drive you crazy to think like that. It's all messed up, that's all I know . . . It used to be you could live okay . . . But now . . .

BILLY: *finishing with the bandaid*
Well, that oughta do it.

RENE:

Yeah, thanks.

BILLY: *putting on his boots*
Yeah, well, maybe we'll find something better, eh? Can't find anything worse.

RENE:

Yeah. You better go now, eh?

BILLY:

What are you gonna tell the cops?

RENE:

Something. I'll tell them something.

BILLY:

Yeah, well . . .

RENE:
Well . . .

BILLY:
Take care, Rene.

RENE:
Yeah, Billy. You too.

BILLY exits.

The noise of the party upstairs is heard.

Slow fade.

TALONBOOKS — PLAYS IN PRINT 1976

Colours in the Dark — James Reaney
The Ecstasy of Rita Joe — George Ryga
Captives of the Faceless Drummer — George Ryga
Crabdance — Beverley Simons
Listen to the Wind — James Reaney
Ashes for Easter & Other Monodramas — David Watmough
Esker Mike & His Wife, Agiluk — Herschel Hardin
Sunrise on Sarah — George Ryga
Walsh — Sharon Pollock
Apple Butter & Other Plays for Children — James Reaney
The Factory Lab Anthology — Connie Brissenden, ed.
The Trial of Jean-Baptiste M. — Robert Gurik
Battering Ram — David Freeman
Hosanna — Michel Tremblay
Les Belles Soeurs — Michel Tremblay
API 2967 — Robert Gurik
You're Gonna Be Alright Jamie Boy — David Freeman
Bethune — Rod Langley
Preparing — Beverley Simons
Forever Yours Marie-Lou — Michel Tremblay
En Pièces Détachées — Michel Tremblay
Lulu Street — Ann Henry
Three Plays by Eric Nicol — Eric Nicol
Fifteen Miles of Broken Glass — Tom Hendry
Bonjour, là, Bonjour — Michel Tremblay
Jacob's Wake — Michael Cook
On the Job — David Fennario
Sqrieux-de-Dieu — Betty Lambert
Some Angry Summer Songs — John Herbert
The Execution — Marie-Claire Blais
Tiln & Other Plays — Michael Cook
Great Wave of Civilization — Herschel Hardin
La Duchesse de Langeais & Other Plays — Michel Tremblay
Have — Julius Hay